Root and Wings

The Art of Raising Mindful, Whole-Hearted Children

Joy Hafner
TrueJoy Publishing

COPYRIGHT PAGE

Root and Wings: The Art of Raising Mindful, Whole-Hearted Children

This book is published by:
TrueJoy Publishing
Author: Joy Hafner
Publisher: TrueJoy Publishing
ISBN: 978-1-971164-22-9
ISBN: 978-1-971164-44-1
Cover design by TrueJoy Publishing
Interior design by TrueJoy Publishing
Printed in the United States of America
First Edition

DEDICATION

To the parents who choose presence over perfection,
healing over habit,
and love as a daily practice.

A Letter to the Reader

Dear Parent, Caregiver, and Fellow Human,

If this book found its way to you, it is likely because something inside you already knows that love can be lived more gently.

You may be reading this while holding a sleeping child, or after a long day when patience felt thin. You may be reading with hope, with exhaustion, with questions, or with a quiet ache to do things differently than they were done for you.

Wherever you are — you belong here.

This book was not written to tell you how to parent. It was written to remind you that you are already capable of raising children with presence, integrity, and heart.

You do not need to be healed before you begin. You do not need to have it all figured out. You only need to be willing to notice, to pause, and to return.

Just because you were raised a certain way does not mean it was right. And just because something was familiar does not mean it was healthy.

Many of us were raised by people who loved us deeply and still passed along patterns shaped by survival, fear, or unhealed pain. That does not make them bad. And it does not make us broken.

It makes us the turning point.

Parenthood invites us into one of the most sacred forms of responsibility: to tend our own inner world so our children do not have to carry it for us.

Your child does not need to understand you. It is not their job to hold your story, manage your emotions, or make sense of your wounds.

Your work is to hold yourself with honesty and compassion —
so your child is free to be exactly who they came here to be.

I believe children are souls before they are roles.
I believe they arrive with their own timing, temperament, and wisdom.
And I believe parents are chosen — not because they are perfect, but because they are capable of
growing.

You will make mistakes. You will lose your patience at times. You will forget what you intended
and remember later.

That remembering is where love lives.

Every repair matters.
Every pause matters.
Every time you choose connection over control, something old loosens and something new takes root.

If this book offers you anything, let it be this:

You are not behind.
You are not failing.
You are not meant to do this perfectly.

You are meant to do it consciously.

May you trust yourself more deeply.
May you soften where you once braced.
May your home become a place where feelings are welcome, boundaries are kind, and love is steady.

And may you remember — on the days when it feels hardest —
that raising a child is also an invitation to raise yourself with the care you may not have received.

With love and gratitude for the work you are doing,
for the courage it takes to break cycles,
and for the light you are choosing to protect,

Joy

TABLE OF CONTENTS

PART I — ROOTS

The Gardeners of Light

Lessons for Parents & Caretakers

1. **The Child as Mirror**
   How Children Reflect Our Energy, Healing, and Presence

2. **Presence Over Perfection**
   Why Repair, Not Perfection, Builds Emotional Safety

3. **Energy Awareness in the Home**
   Creating Calm, Safe, and Nourishing Emotional Environments

4. **The Language of Wonder**
   How Imagination, Story, and Curiosity Shape the Inner World

5. **Boundaries as Love**
   Gentle Structure, Clear Limits, and Emotional Trust

6. **Raising Empaths in a Busy World**
   Sensitivity, Strength, and the Art of Observing Without Absorbing

7. **The Inner Child Link**
   Healing Yourself to Raise Confident, Secure Children

8. **The Sacred Influence of Parents**
   Mothers, Fathers, and the Emotional Templates We Leave Behind
   (Including: The Role of the Father for Daughters • The Mother's Influence on Sons)

9. **The TrueJoy Way**
   Daily Rhythms, Rituals, and Living Mindfulness as a Family

---

PART II — WINGS

The Book of Little Lights

Stories for Children (and the Child Within)

10. **The Day the Stars Spoke**
    Remembering That We Are Made of Love and Light

11. **The Breath Dragon**
    Calming Big Feelings Through Breath and Imagination

12. **The River That Remembered**
    Letting Feelings Flow and Finding Peace Again

13. **The Seed and the Sunbeam**
    Trusting Growth, Patience, and Divine Timing

14. **The Mirror in the Forest**
    Seeing Your Own Light and Loving Yourself Fully

15. **The Invisible Wings**
    Believing in Your Gifts Before You Can See Them

PART III — ROOTS & WINGS TOGETHER

Magic We Make Together

Shared Family Rituals, Games, and Practices

16. **Love in Motion**
    An Invitation to Practice Presence Together

17. **Family Rituals for Grounding and Joy**
    Gratitude, Breath, Emotional Safety, and Connection
    (Includes: The Joy Jar • Lotus Breath Game • Energy Detectives • Morning Magic Minutes)

18. **Creative Practices for Expression and Wonder**
    Art, Dreams, Imagination, and Play
    (Includes: Dream Drawing Nights • Family Affirmation Mural)

19. **Rituals for Regulation, Repair, and Trust**
    Calm, Communication, and Coming Back to Love
    (Includes: Candle of Calm • Feather of Truth • Heart-to-Heart Huddles)

Integration & Closing Blessing

Living the Light, Together
  Raising a Mindful Lineage • Returning to Love • A Blessing for Families

Final Affirmation

We are rooted in love.
We are free to grow.
We rise together.

Introduction

Roots and Wings
Grounding Our Children • Honoring Lineage • Encouraging the Soul to Fly

Roots and Wings

Every child arrives carrying light.

Not because they are perfect—but because they are whole.

Before the world teaches them who to be, before expectations take shape, before fear or comparison or pressure settles in, children know themselves as feeling, sensing, curious beings. They trust their inner world. They move freely between wonder and rest. They love without strategy.

*Our work as parents is not to mold that light—but to **protect it**.*

This book was born from a simple truth many parents feel but don't always have language for:

Just because a way of being was familiar does not always mean it was nourishing. And just because something was widely accepted does not mean it supported emotional safety or inner wholeness.

Many of us were raised by people who loved us deeply and did the best they could with what they knew.
And still, love can coexist with patterns that no longer serve.
Parenthood offers us the chance not to erase the past, but to grow beyond it.

Parenting is not about repeating the past.
It is about choosing what continues—and what ends.

Roots: What We Ground Them In

Roots are what hold a child steady inside themselves.

They are emotional safety.
Nervous system regulation.
Belonging.
Boundaries that say, "You are safe here."

Roots also carry lineage.

They include the ways we were loved—and the ways we weren't.
The patterns we inherited unconsciously.
The reactions that live in the body long after the story is forgotten.

To give our children strong roots, we must be willing to look honestly at our own.

This does not require blame.
It requires awareness.

Our children are not here to understand us, manage us, or heal us.
They are not responsible for our emotions, our history, or our unprocessed pain.

That work belongs to us.

When we heal, regulate, and lead ourselves, we give our children something priceless:
a nervous system that learns safety instead of survival.

Wings: What We Encourage Them To Become

Wings are the invitation to expand.

They are imagination, creativity, intuition, and joy.
They are the freedom to feel deeply without losing oneself.
They are the courage to lead with empathy—not self-abandonment.

Many children today are sensitive, empathic, and perceptive beyond their years.
This is not a flaw—it is a gift.

But sensitivity without guidance can turn into overwhelm.
Empathy without boundaries can become self-erasure.

A child who absorbs everyone else's feelings learns too early that love means fixing, carrying, or pleasing.

This book teaches a different way.

We can raise children who:

- *observe without absorbing*
- *care without carrying*
- *feel deeply without losing their center*
- *lead with kindness and clarity*

These are not doormats.
These are grounded leaders.

Parenting as a Soul-to-Soul Relationship

Many parents feel—whether they name it or not—that children arrive with intention.
That there is something sacred in the pairing.

Some traditions say children choose their parents before birth.
Others simply recognize the unmistakable sense of purpose that arrives with a child.

You do not have to take this literally for it to be meaningful.

What matters is this:

Your child did not come to you for perfection.
They came for presence.
For growth.
For the possibility of something new.

And you did not stop being a soul when you became a parent.

You are still becoming, still healing, still remembering.

Parenting, at its most conscious, is not a hierarchy—it is a relationship between souls at different stages of remembering who they are.

The Art of Raising Whole-Hearted Children

This book is not a manual for perfect parenting.

It is an invitation into **artful parenting**—
where rhythm matters more than rigidity,
repair matters more than performance,
and love is something practiced daily, not promised abstractly.

Inside these pages you will find:

- *guidance for parents and caretakers*
- *stories written for children's hearts*
- *shared rituals that turn ordinary moments into anchors of safety and wonder*

*Together, they form a way of living that grounds children deeply **and** allows them to fly.*

A Quiet Promise

If you offer your child roots—
safety, boundaries, presence, and truth—

and you offer them wings—
wonder, imagination, trust, and encouragement—

they will not lose themselves in the world.

They will meet it whole.

This is the art of raising mindful, whole-hearted children.

Not by being perfect.
But by being present.

Welcome to Root and Wings.

PART I — ROOTS

The Gardeners of Light

Chapter One

The Child as Mirror

How Children Reflect Our Energy, Healing, and Presence

Story Insight

One afternoon, I watched a mother and her young son at the park.
The child ran freely at first—laughing, tumbling, climbing higher with each burst of courage.
Each time he stumbled, the mother gasped. Her body tightened. She rushed toward him before he had even decided whether he needed help.

After a few minutes, the boy stopped running.

He stayed close.
His laughter softened.
His body, once expansive, became cautious.

Nothing had been said.
But everything had been felt.

Children do not experience us primarily through words.
They experience us through **energy, tone, breath, and presence**.

They feel our nervous systems before they understand our rules.
They read our unspoken fears before they hear our reassurances.

This is not because they are fragile.
It is because they are exquisitely perceptive.

Teaching

Children are mirrors—not in a way that accuses us, but in a way that reveals.

They reflect:

- how safe the world feels in our bodies
- how we respond to stress
- how we relate to emotion
- how we treat ourselves when things go wrong

When a child becomes reactive, withdrawn, overly compliant, or emotionally heightened, it is rarely because they are "being difficult."

More often, they are responding to the **emotional climate** around them.

This does not mean parents must be calm all the time. It means children learn safety not from perfection—but from **regulation and repair**.

A regulated adult nervous system becomes the child's first teacher of peace.

When we pause instead of react, the child learns pause.
When we breathe instead of escalate, the child learns breathing.
When we repair instead of shame, the child learns that love does not disappear during mistakes.

Roots Begin in the Body

Before children understand logic, they understand **felt sense**.

They know:

- whether love is steady or conditional
- whether emotions are safe or disruptive
- whether mistakes lead to connection or rejection

This is why early childhood is not about instruction—it is about embodiment.

Roots form when a child experiences:

- predictable care
- emotional availability
- calm leadership
- loving limits

These roots are not built by explaining emotions, but by **modeling how emotions are lived with**.

A Gentle Truth

Our children are not here to manage us.
They are not here to understand our stress, our past, or our unhealed places.

Many of us were taught—subtly or overtly—to read the room, anticipate needs, soften ourselves, or stay quiet to keep peace.
That learning often began in childhood.

Root and Wings offers another way.

We can choose to be the adults in the room—steady enough that children do not need to become so.

This is not about being perfect.
It is about being **responsible for our inner state**.

When Triggers Appear

Parenting has a way of awakening old memories in the body.

A child's defiance may stir our own fear of being "too much."
A tantrum may echo moments when big feelings were not allowed.
A child's joy may even awaken grief for the freedom we lost too early.

These moments are not failures.
They are invitations.

Each trigger is an opportunity to pause and ask:
What is being stirred in me right now?

When we respond from awareness instead of reflex, the cycle begins to change.

Parent Practice — The Mirror Moment

The next time your child's behavior activates you, try this:

1. Pause before responding.
2. Place one hand on your chest.
3. Take three slow breaths, extending the exhale.

4. Silently say:
    "This moment is information, not accusation."

5. Ask yourself:
    "What does my child need right now—and what do I need to regulate before offering it?"

Then respond from that grounded place.

This practice alone can transform countless moments.

Reflection Prompts

- When my child expresses big emotions, what happens in my body first?

- What behaviors trigger me most strongly—and what might they be mirroring?

- How was emotion handled in my childhood home?

- What would it feel like to meet my child's emotions with curiosity instead of urgency?

Closing Thought

Children do not need parents who never struggle.
They need parents who are willing to notice, soften, and return.

When we tend our own inner state, we give our children the deepest root of all:

the felt experience of safety in relationship.

And from that root, everything else grows.

Chapter Two

Presence Over Perfection

Why Repair, Not Flawlessness, Builds Emotional Safety

Story Insight

A parent once said to me, "I just want to get it right every time."

There was love in their voice.
And exhaustion.

Many parents carry the quiet belief that good parenting means fewer mistakes, calmer reactions, better answers, and constant emotional availability. The bar keeps rising, and the nervous system never rests.

But children are not measuring our performance.
They are sensing our **availability**.

They will forget the perfectly planned activity.
They will remember whether we were emotionally there.

One evening, after a long day, I snapped at my child over something small. His face fell—not in fear, but in confusion. I saw it immediately. I sat down beside him and said, "I was tired and reacted too quickly. That wasn't fair. I'm sorry."

He leaned into me and said, "It's okay. I still love you."

In that moment, something rewired—not just for him, but for me.

Teaching

Perfection is fear dressed as responsibility.
Presence is trust dressed as love.

Children do not need parents who never lose patience.
They need parents who **return**.

Neuroscience tells us that **repair** is more important than regulation done "right" the first time. When a parent notices a misstep and reconnects with warmth, the child's brain learns something vital:

- Love is stable.
- Conflict does not equal abandonment.
- Mistakes can be mended.

This is how emotional resilience is built.

When perfection is the goal, children learn pressure.
When presence is the practice, children learn safety.

Roots Grow in Repair

Every family experiences moments of disconnection.
What shapes a child is not the rupture—it is the repair.

Repair looks like:

- apologizing without over-explaining
- naming emotions without blaming
- reconnecting without shame

A simple, sincere "I'm sorry, I was overwhelmed" teaches far more than silence ever could.

It shows a child:

- accountability without self-attack
- emotional honesty without collapse
- strength that includes softness

These moments form roots that say, "I can be imperfect and still be loved."

Letting Go of the Ideal Parent

Many parents are parenting against something:

- "I'll never be like my mother."
- "I won't repeat what I went through."
- "My child will never feel how I felt."

While the intention is loving, this can quietly create rigidity.

Healing does not require opposition—it requires **integration**.

You are allowed to:

- learn as you go
- change your mind
- pause mid-sentence
- try again

Children don't need you to be an ideal.
They need you to be **real and regulated enough to lead**.

Wings Grow in Witnessing Humanity

When children see us acknowledge our humanity with kindness, they learn to do the same.

They learn:

- self-compassion
- emotional literacy
- flexibility
- forgiveness

A child who watches a parent recover from a hard moment learns that emotions move, relationships endure, and repair is possible.

This becomes a wing they will carry into friendships, partnerships, and parenthood of their own.

Parent Practice — The Presence Reset

When you notice yourself slipping into "I should be doing better," try this:

1. Stop what you're doing.
2. Name one thing you appreciate about your child in that moment.
3. Make eye contact and soften your face.
4. Say silently or aloud:
   "Right now is enough."
5. Take one slow breath before continuing.

This resets your nervous system and brings you back into relationship.

Reflection Prompts

- Where do I place the most pressure on myself as a parent?
- How was imperfection treated in my childhood home?
- What does repair look like in my family right now?
- How might my child benefit from seeing me apologize or pause?

Closing Thought

Children are not looking for flawless parents.
They are looking for **present ones**.

Presence says:
"I am here."
"I can return."
"Love doesn't leave when things get messy."

From that knowing, roots deepen.
From that safety, wings begin to stretch.

Chapter Three

Energy Awareness in the Home

Creating Calm, Safe, and Nourishing Emotional Environments

Story Insight

When my child was small, he once walked into the living room, paused, and said, "Mom, it feels loud in here."

No one was talking.
The television was off.
Nothing appeared out of place.

But the room was loud—with unspoken tension, rushed movement, and a day that had not yet been exhaled.

Children often feel the atmosphere of a space long before they can explain it. They sense when adults are distracted, emotionally charged, or carrying unresolved stress. They notice tone shifts, hurried footsteps, and the absence of ease.

Not because they are fragile—but because they are attuned.

Teaching

A home is more than a physical structure.
It is an emotional ecosystem.

Every interaction leaves a trace:

- how we speak to one another
- how we recover from stress
- how conflict is held or avoided
- how rest is honored—or not

Children learn what "normal" feels like not from what we tell them, but from what they live inside.

Energy awareness does not mean creating a perfectly calm home.
Emotion is part of life.

Energy awareness means knowing **how emotion moves**, and how quickly safety can be restored.

Roots Grow in Felt Safety

Before children understand rules or reasoning, they ask one essential question with their bodies:

"Am I safe here?"

Safety is communicated through:

- predictable rhythms
- calm voices during stress
- emotional repair after conflict
- adults who can regulate themselves

A child does not need a quiet house.
They need a house that **returns to calm**.

When tension rises and then resolves, children learn:

- feelings are temporary
- conflict is survivable
- peace is accessible again

These lessons form roots that anchor resilience.

Reading the Emotional Climate

You can begin building awareness by simply noticing.

Ask yourself:

- How does my body feel when I walk into my home?
- Do I exhale, or brace?
- What emotions linger in shared spaces?

Notice pace:

- Are mornings rushed or rhythmic?
- Do evenings allow for decompression?

Notice sound:

- Is there constant stimulation, or moments of quiet?
- What sounds help everyone settle—music, silence, laughter?

This is not about judgment.
It is about information.

Children as Natural Regulators

Children often attempt to regulate environments instinctively.

They may:

- withdraw into their room
- line up toys or objects
- hum, rock, or repeat phrases
- become extra playful or extra quiet

These behaviors are not misbehavior—they are attempts at balance.

When we see them this way, we can support regulation rather than correct it.

Gentle Ways to Restore Balance

Energy awareness becomes powerful when it is paired with simple, repeatable practices.

Morning Light Reset
Open curtains or a window each morning.
Let natural light touch the room.
Say quietly or aloud:
"We begin again today."

The Emotional Weather Check
Invite everyone to name how they feel using simple imagery:
sunny, cloudy, stormy, calm.
No fixing—just noticing.

Breath Breaks

When tension rises, pause together for three slow breaths.
This teaches that calm is something we return to, not something we demand.

Evening Release

Before bed, invite the day to end.
Name one thing to let go of and one thing to appreciate.

These small practices tell a child's nervous system:
"This home knows how to settle."

Wings Grow in Emotional Literacy

When children grow up in homes where emotions are noticed but not feared, they learn:

- how to name what they feel
- how to release rather than store tension
- how to stay present without absorbing others' stress

They do not become emotionally numb.
They become emotionally wise.

This is how sensitivity becomes strength rather than overwhelm.

Parent Practice — The Evening Reset

At the end of the day, try this simple practice:

1. Stand or sit quietly in a shared space.
2. Place one hand on your heart.
3. Take three slow breaths.
4. Ask yourself silently:
   "What energy do I want to release from today?"
5. Exhale it gently.
6. Whisper:
   "Peace returns here."

You don't need to explain this to your child.
They will feel it.

Reflection Prompts

- What emotional tone did I grow up around?
- How does my home feel when I enter it now?
- What helps my family return to calm most easily?
- How might slowing down change the energy we live inside?

Closing Thought

A mindful home is not a quiet one.
It is a responsive one.

When children grow up in spaces that acknowledge emotion and know how to restore balance, they develop a deep inner trust:

No matter what happens, I can come back to myself.

That trust becomes a root strong enough to support any wing.

Chapter Four

The Language of Wonder

How Imagination, Curiosity, and Story Shape the Inner World

Story Insight

One evening, a child pointed to the sky and said,
 "The moon followed us home."

The parent smiled, nodded, and replied,
 "Yes, it likes you."

Nothing more needed to be explained.

In that moment, wonder was protected.

Children speak a language long before they master words.
It is the language of imagination — a way of understanding life that blends feeling, curiosity, and meaning.

Through this language, children make sense of emotions too large for logic and ideas too subtle for explanation.

When we rush to correct, rationalize, or dismiss wonder, we don't just end a conversation — we close a doorway.

Teaching

Imagination is not an escape from reality.
It is how children enter it.

Before a child can articulate self-worth, they feel it through play.
Before they can name intuition, they experience it through story.
Before they understand meaning, they live inside metaphor.

Wonder is the mind in an open state.
It is curiosity without fear.

When imagination is welcomed, children learn that their inner world is trustworthy.

Roots Grow When Wonder Is Safe

Children do not need to be taught how to imagine.
They need to be shown that imagination is **allowed**.

Roots deepen when:

- curiosity is met with patience
- questions are welcomed without urgency
- stories are explored without needing a lesson attached

A child who feels safe to imagine feels safe to be.

This safety becomes an internal root:
My inner world matters.

The Parent's Role as Listener

You do not need to create wonder.
You need to **receive it**.

When a child tells you a story that makes no sense to adult logic, they are not asking for accuracy — they are asking for presence.

Try responding with:

- "Tell me more."
- "What happened next?"
- "How did that feel?"

These responses tell the child:
Your inner world is welcome here.

Words Carry Energy

Children absorb tone before meaning.

Words spoken with curiosity expand.
Words spoken with dismissal contract.

Small shifts matter:

- "That's silly" becomes "That's interesting."
- "That's not real" becomes "What do you imagine?"
- "Stop pretending" becomes "Tell me about it."

Language shapes reality — especially in developing nervous systems.

When Wonder Begins to Fade

Wonder doesn't disappear because children grow older.
It fades when it is repeatedly rushed, corrected, or ignored.

Performance-heavy environments, overstimulation, and constant evaluation teach children to prioritize output over presence.

To restore wonder:

- slow transitions
- allow boredom
- spend time outdoors
- tell stories without outcomes

Wonder returns quickly when space is offered.

Wings Grow Through Imagination

Imagination teaches children to:

- see possibilities
- empathize with others
- hold multiple perspectives
- trust inner guidance

These are not soft skills.
They are leadership skills.

Children who keep their wonder intact grow into adults who innovate, empathize, and imagine better futures.

Parent Practice — The Three-Minute Story

Once a day, invite shared imagination.

1. Begin a story with one sentence:
   "Once there was a little light who felt…"
2. Let your child continue the next sentence.
3. Take turns adding one line at a time.
4. Let the story end wherever it ends.

No lesson required.

The connection is the teaching.

Reflection Prompts

- How was imagination treated in my childhood?
- Do I rush to explain or allow mystery?
- When do I feel most curious or playful?
- What happens in my body when I slow down with my child's wonder?

Closing Thought

Wonder is not something children outgrow.
It is something they are taught to abandon.

When we protect a child's imagination, we protect their ability to feel meaning, connection, and possibility. These are wings the world cannot take from them.

Chapter Five

Boundaries as Love

How Structure Creates Safety, Freedom, and Trust

Story Insight

A little boy once said to his parent,
"You're my fence."

The parent paused, unsure how to respond.

The child continued,
"You keep me safe, but I can still see everything."

Children understand boundaries long before they can explain them.
They do not experience loving limits as rejection — they experience them as relief.

Uncertainty, not structure, is what creates anxiety.

When limits are unclear, children must constantly scan their environment to figure out what is allowed, what is expected, and where safety begins and ends.

Boundaries quiet that scan.

Teaching

Boundaries are not walls meant to shut children in.
They are containers that allow children to relax inside themselves.

A loving boundary says:

- I am paying attention.
- I will guide you.
- You do not have to manage this alone.

Children raised without boundaries often feel overwhelmed, not free.
Children raised with rigid control feel constrained, not safe.

The balance is found in **clear, calm leadership**.

Roots Grow Through Consistency

Consistency builds trust.

When boundaries are predictable and compassionate, children learn:

- what to expect
- how to regulate themselves
- where responsibility lives

This consistency creates internal roots:
The world makes sense. I am held.

Roots are strengthened not by strictness, but by steadiness.

Connection Before Correction

Before behavior can change, emotion must be acknowledged.

A child in distress cannot access logic.
Their nervous system must feel seen first.

Try this order:

1. **Name the feeling** — "I see you're upset."
2. **State the boundary** — "I can't let you hit."
3. **Offer direction** — "You can stomp your feet or ask for help."

This sequence teaches regulation without shame.

Boundaries Teach Self-Respect

Boundaries are not only about safety — they teach children how to treat themselves and others.

When children see limits delivered with calm clarity, they learn:

- saying no does not end connection
- expressing needs is allowed
- power does not require aggression

These lessons grow wings:
children who respect their own limits become adults who lead with integrity.

When Boundaries Become Control

It's important to notice when boundaries are serving fear instead of love.

Signs a boundary may need reevaluation:

- it is enforced through intimidation or shame
- it exists primarily to soothe adult anxiety
- it does not evolve as the child grows

A helpful question is:
Is this limit about protection, or about control?

Boundaries rooted in love grow with the child.

Repair Is Part of Boundary-Setting

Every parent will set a limit imperfectly at times.

What matters is repair.

"I was too harsh earlier. Let's try that again."
"I raised my voice. I'm sorry."

These moments show children:

- authority can be accountable
- power can be kind
- love remains even when mistakes happen

This models healthy leadership.

Parent Practice — The Loving Limit

When setting a boundary, try this:

1. Lower yourself to your child's level.
2. Make eye contact.
3. Place one hand on your heart.
4. State the limit clearly and calmly.
5. End with reassurance:
   "I'm here with you."

One calm repetition is more effective than many emotional ones.

Reflection Prompts

- How were boundaries handled in my childhood home?
- Do I tend toward rigidity or avoidance when setting limits?
- What boundaries help my child feel safest?
- How can my limits evolve as my child grows?

Closing Thought

Boundaries are not the opposite of love.
 They are love, expressed through leadership.

When children are held by clear, compassionate limits, they grow rooted in trust —
and free enough to stretch their wings.

.

Chapter Six

Raising Empaths in a Busy World

How Sensitivity Becomes Strength—and Boundaries Become Power

Story Insight

When my child was small, he could sense tension before anyone spoke.

If someone nearby was upset, he would immediately offer comfort—his favorite toy, a hug, a joke. His instinct was generous and tender. But it came with a cost.

One day after school, he sat quietly, shoulders heavy.
When I asked what was wrong, he said,
"I tried to make her happy, but now I feel sad."

In that moment, I understood something essential:

Empathy without guidance becomes absorption.
And absorption, over time, becomes exhaustion.

Sensitive children do not need to feel less.
They need to feel **wisely**.

Teaching

Empathy is one of the greatest forms of intelligence.

Empathic children perceive emotional shifts, unspoken feelings, and subtle energy. They often care deeply, notice quickly, and respond instinctively.

But in a world that is loud, fast, and emotionally charged, empathy without boundaries can become overwhelming.

There is an important distinction every empathic child must learn:

To observe is healthy.
To absorb is harmful.

Unhealed empathy says:

- If someone is hurting, I must fix it.
- If someone is upset, it's my fault.
- If I say no, I might lose love.

Healed empathy says:

- I can care without carrying.
- I can witness without taking on.
- I can be kind and still stay whole.

Our role as parents is to help children make this shift early.

Roots Grow Through Emotional Ownership

Many empathic children unconsciously take responsibility for the emotional state of others.

They learn to:

- read the room
- anticipate reactions
- adjust themselves to keep peace

This pattern often forms not because parents are unloving—but because children sense vulnerability and respond instinctively.

Without guidance, this can wire the nervous system toward people-pleasing, anxiety, and self-abandonment.

Roots strengthen when children learn:

- My feelings belong to me.
- Other people's feelings belong to them.
- I am allowed to take up space.

This is not selfishness.
It is emotional clarity.

Teaching Children to Observe, Not Absorb

This distinction can be taught simply and gently.

Name the Difference
When your child says, "I feel weird," ask:
"Is that your feeling, or did you pick it up from someone else?"

This builds emotional awareness without judgment.

Create a Visual Boundary
Invite your child to imagine a soft light or bubble around their body.
Explain:
"This light lets love in, but other people's feelings don't have to stick."

Make it playful—superhero shields, glowing wings, invisible cloaks.

Model Ownership
Say aloud:
"I'm feeling frustrated, and that's mine to take care of."
This teaches that empathy does not require absorption.

Boundaries Are Not Unkind

Many sensitive children fear that boundaries will hurt others.

Teach them early:

- Saying no can be loving.
- Rest is not rejection.
- Caring does not require sacrifice of self.

A child who learns this grows into an adult who can lead, guide, and support others **without disappearing**.

These are not doormats.

These are leaders.

Wings Grow When Sensitivity Is Honored

A healed empath:

- feels deeply without drowning
- listens without fixing
- supports without rescuing
- leads with compassion and clarity

When children are taught to trust their sensitivity and protect it, their empathy becomes a stabilizing force in the world.

They become the calm ones in chaos.
The steady ones in crisis.
The kind ones who do not lose themselves.

Parent Practice — The Empath Reset

After an emotionally intense day, try this together:

1. Shake arms and legs gently, like shaking off rain.
2. Take a slow breath in through the nose.
3. Exhale through the mouth, imagining anything heavy leaving the body.
4. Say together:
    "I send back what is not mine with kindness."
    "I keep my own peace."
5. End with a hug or grounding touch.

This practice teaches release, not suppression.

Reflection Prompts

- How was sensitivity treated in my childhood?
- Do I model emotional ownership or over-responsibility?
- What boundaries help my child stay regulated?
- How can I affirm my child's empathy while teaching self-protection?

Closing Thought

Sensitivity is not a burden to manage.
It is a gift to be guided.

When children learn to observe without absorbing, care without carrying, and love without losing themselves, they grow into adults who change the world gently—but powerfully.

These are the wings that rise from strong roots.

Chapter Seven

The Inner Child Link

Healing Yourself to Raise Confident, Secure Children

Story Insight

One afternoon, my child spilled a cup of paint across the floor.

The sound alone stirred something sharp in my body — a familiar tightening, a rush of words that had not yet formed. I recognized it immediately. That reaction didn't belong to this moment.

I paused.

Instead of responding from habit, I softened my shoulders and said,
"It's okay. Accidents happen. Let's clean it up together."

My child relaxed.
And so did something inside me.

In that quiet moment, I realized something important:
every time we choose presence over reaction, **two children are being cared for —**
the one in front of us, and the one still living inside us.

Teaching

Becoming a parent has a way of waking up memories stored not in the mind, but in the body.

Moments with our children can echo moments from our own childhood:

- a raised voice
- a look of disappointment
- emotional silence
- feeling misunderstood

This is not a flaw in parenting. It is an invitation.

Our children do not cause these reactions — they reveal them.

And when revealed with awareness, they can finally be met with compassion.

Roots Grow Through Self-Compassion

The inner child is not something to analyze or fix.

It is the part of us that learned early how to adapt, survive, and belong.

When unacknowledged, it may:

- react quickly
- avoid conflict
- over-explain
- struggle to set boundaries

When cared for, it becomes a bridge to empathy, patience, and play.

Healing does not mean reliving the past.
It means responding differently in the present.

Every time you pause instead of react, your nervous system learns a new path —
and your child's nervous system learns safety.

Breaking Cycles Without Blame

Many parents worry they will repeat what they experienced.

Awareness dissolves that fear.

Cycles are not broken by effort alone — they are broken by **conscious interruption**.

That interruption may sound like:

- "That wasn't how I wanted to respond. Let's try again."
- "I need a moment to calm my body before I answer."
- "I was wrong, and I'm still here."

These moments teach children something powerful:

Love is steady.
Authority can be accountable.
Repair is safe.

Projection and Pause

When a reaction feels bigger than the moment, it often is.

Before responding, gently ask yourself:
Whose voice is speaking right now — my adult self, or my younger one?

This question alone creates space.

Space is where choice lives.

And choice is where healing happens.

Wings Grow Through Emotional Honesty

When children witness adults naming emotions without collapsing into them, they learn:

- feelings are safe
- emotions pass
- self-regulation is possible

They do not need parents who never struggle.

They need parents who show that struggle does not erase love.

This honesty gives children permission to be human — and confident in that humanity.

Parent Practice — The Inner Child Pause

When you feel triggered:

1. Place one hand on your chest.
2. Take a slow breath in, longer breath out.
3. Silently say:
   "I am safe. I am the adult now."
4. Respond from that grounded place.

This practice shifts the nervous system from reaction to leadership.

Reflection Prompts

- What situations with my child feel most activating?
- What do those moments remind me of?
- How was emotional expression handled when I was young?
- What does compassion toward myself look like now?

Closing Thought

Healing yourself is not something you do instead of parenting.

It is something you do **for** your child.

Each time you respond with awareness, you change the emotional inheritance your child receives.

That is how roots strengthen — and how wings learn to trust the sky.

Chapter Eight

The Sacred Influence of Parents

How Mothers, Fathers, and Caregivers Shape Safety, Identity, and Love

Story Insight

A young girl once asked her father,
"Is it okay if I'm loud?"

He smiled and said,
"Yes. You don't need to make yourself smaller for the world."

Years later, she would remember that moment—not because of the words alone,
but because her body felt permission.

Children are always learning who they are allowed to be by watching how the adults
closest to them relate to themselves, to one another, and to the child.

Parenting is not only what we teach.
It is what we model.

Teaching

Every child learns about love, safety, power, and worth through relationship.

The adults who raise them become the first mirrors for:

- how affection is expressed
- how conflict is handled
- how emotions are respected
- how boundaries are honored

This influence is not about perfection or prescribed roles.
It is about **presence, respect, and emotional integrity**.

Whether in two-parent homes, single-parent families, blended families, or chosen family systems, children learn through consistent relational energy.

What matters most is not who fills the role—but **how it is held**.

Roots Grow Through Relational Safety

Children feel safest when the adults around them:

- communicate with respect
- repair after conflict
- hold steady emotional leadership
- allow feelings without overwhelm

When children witness adults navigating disagreement without fear, they learn that love does not fracture under pressure.

This creates roots that say:
Connection is reliable. I don't have to choose between honesty and belonging.

The Influence of the Masculine Presence

For many children—especially daughters—the presence of a grounded, respectful masculine figure shapes their sense of safety in the world.

A healthy masculine presence teaches:

- steadiness without dominance
- protection without control
- confidence without aggression

When a child experiences masculine energy that is calm, present, and emotionally available, they learn:
I am safe to be myself. I am worthy of respect.

This influence is not limited to biological fathers.
 It can come from any caregiver who embodies grounded leadership and emotional reliability.

The Influence of the Feminine Presence

For many children—especially sons—the presence of a nurturing, emotionally attuned feminine figure shapes their understanding of tenderness and care.

A healthy feminine presence teaches:

- empathy without self-sacrifice
- nurturing without enmeshment
- emotional expression without shame

When a child experiences feminine energy that is both nurturing and steady, they learn that love can be generous without self-sacrifice.

Again, this influence transcends biology.
It is about emotional tone and relational presence.

Modeling Respect Between Adults

Perhaps the most powerful lesson children receive is how adults treat one another.

Children learn about partnership by watching:

- how voices are raised or softened
- how apologies are offered
- how differences are respected

They absorb:

- what love looks like under stress
- whether power is shared or controlled
- whether repair is possible

Even in households where adults are no longer together, respect remains a teacher.
A child who witnesses dignity in separation learns resilience, not loss.

Wings Grow When Children Are Seen Clearly

When parents see children as whole beings—not extensions, not reflections of unmet dreams—children learn autonomy.

They learn:

- their feelings matter
- their voice is welcome
- their individuality is honored

This gives wings not of rebellion, but of confidence.

Children who feel respected do not need to fight for identity—they grow into it.

Parent Practice — Modeling in Real Time

Choose one moment each day to consciously model what you hope your child learns.

It may be:

- pausing before reacting
- setting a boundary kindly
- expressing appreciation
- repairing after tension

Say aloud when appropriate:
"I'm taking a breath so I can respond with care."

This teaches leadership through transparency.

Reflection Prompts

- What did I learn about love by watching my caregivers?
- How do I model respect during stress or disagreement?
- What qualities do I want my child to recognize as normal in relationships?
- Where can I lead with greater emotional clarity?

Closing Thought

Children do not need perfect role models.

They need **present ones**—adults who are willing to grow, repair, and lead with integrity.

When children are raised in environments where respect is lived, not demanded, they grow rooted in self-worth.

And from that grounding, they rise—free, confident, and whole-hearted.

Chapter Nine

The TrueJoy Way

Living Mindfulness as a Family Rhythm, Not a Rulebook

Story Insight

One morning, my child asked,
"Why do we light a candle when it's already light outside?"

I smiled and said,
"Because light likes to remember itself."

He nodded, satisfied, and went back to his cereal.

That small exchange held everything I believe about mindful parenting.

We are not here to teach our children who to become.
We are here to remind them of what they already are.

And the way we do that is not through perfection, but through **presence woven into daily life**.

Teaching

The TrueJoy Way is not a method.
It is a way of moving through the ordinary with intention.

Children thrive in **rhythm**, not rigidity.

Routine can feel mechanical.
Rhythm feels alive.

A rhythmic family life offers:

- predictability without pressure
- structure without force
- meaning without performance

It allows children's nervous systems to relax because they know what to expect—and that calm always returns.

Roots Grow Through Daily Anchors

Roots are strengthened by small, repeated experiences of safety.

This does not require more time or effort—only attention.

Simple anchors might include:

- a shared breath before the day begins
- a consistent check-in after school
- a gentle closing ritual before sleep

These moments quietly say:
No matter what happens, we come back to one another.

Children raised with daily anchors learn that connection is reliable.

Wings Grow Through Sacred Ordinary Moments

The TrueJoy Way does not separate spirituality from life.

It invites meaning into:

- washing hands
- walking to school
- eating together
- bedtime conversations

When presence is practiced in ordinary moments, children learn that mindfulness is not something we "do"—it is how we live.

This creates wings that are not fragile or performative, but grounded and sustainable.

When the Day Falls Apart

There will be days when the rhythm breaks.

Mornings run late.
Tempers rise.
Everyone is tired.

The TrueJoy Way does not ask you to fix the day.

It asks you to **return**.

Returning may look like:

- a shared breath
- a sincere apology
- a quiet moment of reconnection

Children learn most not from how we begin, but from how we come back together.

A Word About Pressure

Mindfulness should never become another standard to fail.

If a practice is skipped, nothing is lost.
If a ritual is forgotten, love remains.

The most important practice is kindness—toward yourself and toward your child.

Children feel self-compassion before they understand it.

Parent Practice — The Family Light Moment

Once a week, choose a quiet moment together.

Light a candle or simply pause.

Each person shares one way they noticed kindness, effort, or courage—either in themselves or someone else.

End by saying together:
 "We remember the light."

This simple moment reinforces everything the book teaches—without effort.

Reflection Prompts

- What rhythms already support my family's sense of safety?
- Where can I simplify instead of add?
- How do I model returning after stress?
- What does mindful living look like in my real, imperfect life?

Closing Thought

The TrueJoy Way is not about doing more.

It is about **being more present** in what is already here.

When families live this way, children grow up knowing that:

- love is steady
- mistakes are survivable
- peace is accessible

These are roots strong enough to hold any storm.

And from them, wings grow naturally.

The Book of Little Lights

Stories for Children (and the Child Within)

Part II Introduction

For the Children Who Remember

Before children know rules,
they know feeling.

Before they understand words,
they understand tone.

Before they learn who the world expects them to be,
they know who they are.

This section is written for that knowing.

The stories that follow are not lessons in disguise.
They are invitations.

They speak in the language children already understand —
the language of imagination, metaphor, wonder, and quiet truth.

You do not need to explain these stories.
You do not need to correct interpretations or extract meaning.

Simply read.
Simply listen.
Simply be together.

Children take what they need.

And sometimes, so do we.

The Day the Stars Spoke

There was once a child named Lonna who loved the night sky.

Every evening, she would lie on her back and talk to the stars.
She told them about her day — what made her laugh, what made her quiet, what made her wonder.

One night, she asked softly,
 "Why do you shine even when no one is looking?"

The stars shimmered.

For the first time, a gentle voice floated down from the sky.

"Because shining is not something we do," the stars said.
 "It is something we are."

Lonna sat up, surprised.
"Even when it's cloudy?" she asked.

"Even then," the stars replied.
 "Clouds can hide light, but they cannot take it away."

Lonna looked at her hands.
They seemed to glow just a little.

"Does that mean I'm light too?" she whispered.

The stars twinkled brighter.
"Of course. Every kind thought, every brave feeling, every gentle moment — they all travel farther than you can see."

Lonna smiled so wide the moon seemed to smile back.

From that night on, whenever she felt unsure or small, she would look up and remember:

Light does not disappear.
It waits.

Tiny Truth

"I am made of love and light."

Parent & Child Reflection

- Ask gently:
  "What do you think your light feels like today?"

- Optional shared moment:
  Stand together under the night sky (or by a window).
  Take one slow breath and whisper:
  "We remember our light."

- Creative extension (optional):
  Draw or cut out stars and write one kind word or feeling on each.
  Place them somewhere your child can see them before sleep.

The Breath Dragon

High in the blue hills lived a small dragon named Ember.

Ember was kind and curious, but his fire was big.

When he was excited, sparks danced from his nose.
When he felt scared, smoke curled from his ears.
And when he got angry — whoosh — flames burst out before he could stop them.

Ember didn't want to scare anyone.
He just felt too much.

One day, after accidentally singeing a patch of flowers, Ember ran to the lake and hid behind a rock. His chest felt tight. His fire felt stuck.

"I wish I didn't have fire at all," he sniffed.

A slow, steady voice answered,
"Fire isn't the problem, little one."

Ember looked up to see a wise old turtle resting by the water.

"The problem," the turtle continued, "is that you haven't learned how to guide it."

The turtle placed a smooth stone on Ember's belly.

"Breathe in," she said, "and feel the stone rise."

Ember inhaled slowly.
The stone lifted. His fire warmed — but didn't leap.

"Now breathe out," she said, "as if you're blowing a soft cloud instead of a flame."

Ember exhaled. A gentle mist floated into the air.

Something shifted.

His chest softened.
The fire settled into a warm glow.

"See?" smiled the turtle. "Your breath is the path your fire follows."

From that day on, whenever Ember felt his fire grow too big, he would pause and breathe.

And his fire learned how to shine without burning.

Tiny Truth

"My breath helps me feel calm and safe."

Parent & Child Reflection

- Ask gently:
  "When does your fire feel big?"

- Practice together:
  Place a hand on the belly.
  Breathe in slowly through the nose.
  Breathe out slowly through the mouth like blowing a cloud.

- Optional play:
  Pretend to be dragons who blow bubbles or paper streamers using slow breaths.

The River That Remembered

There was once a river named Raya who loved to sing.

She sang as she flowed around stones,
she hummed as she danced past trees,
and every ripple carried her song forward.

One day, heavy rains fell.
Branches, leaves, and mud tumbled into Raya's waters.

She tried to keep singing, but the weight slowed her down.
"I have to hold this all together," Raya thought.
"If I let go, I might disappear."

So, she stopped moving.

The birds grew quiet.
The water became still and cloudy.

A tall heron landed beside her.

"Why have you gone silent?" he asked.

"I'm too full," Raya whispered. "I don't know how to move anymore."

The heron nodded kindly.
"A river is not meant to hold everything," he said.
"It is meant to carry things through."

Raya trembled.
Then slowly, gently, she allowed herself to flow again.

The branches drifted away.
The mud softened.
Her song returned — slower, wiser, but still hers.

Raya smiled as she moved forward, remembering who she was.

Tiny Truth

"My feelings can move through me."

Parent & Child Reflection

- Ask softly:
  "Do some feelings ever feel stuck?"

- Try together:
  Fill a bowl with water and floating leaves.
  Name each leaf after a feeling and gently blow it downstream.

- Reassure:
  "It's safe to feel, and it's safe to let go."

The Seed and the Sunbeam

Deep in the soil lived a tiny seed named Soli.

Soli dreamed of becoming a tall sunflower.
Every morning, she listened for the birds and whispered,
"Is today the day?"

The rain came.
The soil stayed dark.
Nothing seemed to happen.

"Maybe I'm forgotten," Soli sighed.

A warm voice drifted down through the earth.

"I'm here," said the Sunbeam.
"I've been with you the whole time."

"But I can't see you," Soli said.
"And I'm not growing."

The Sunbeam laughed softly.
"Growth begins where you cannot see it. Roots come before petals."

Soli rested.
She stretched quietly in the dark.
Days passed.

Then one morning, she felt herself reaching upward — breaking through the soil
into light.

She turned her face to the sky.

"You never left," she said.

"Never," replied the Sunbeam.
"I was inside you all along."

Tiny Truth

"I grow in my own time."

Parent & Child Reflection

- Ask gently:
  "Is there something you're waiting to grow?"

- Try together:
  Plant a seed and care for it each day.
  Whisper, "Roots first, wings later."

- Reassure:
  "Even when we can't see it, growth is happening."

The Mirror in the Forest

At the edge of a quiet forest stood a tall silver tree.

Its bark was smooth and shiny, like a mirror made of moonlight.

One afternoon, a child named Leo wandered into the forest, following the sound of birdsong. When he reached the silver tree, he stopped.

Someone was standing there.

It looked just like him.

Leo smiled.
The reflection smiled back.

He frowned.
The reflection frowned too.

He waved, jumped, and made silly faces — and the mirror did the same.

"This is strange," Leo said. "You only copy me. You don't tell me who I am."

A soft breeze moved through the leaves.

The tree spoke gently,
 "I am not here to tell you who you are. I am here to show you."

Leo tilted his head.
 "Show me what?"

"When you smile," said the tree, "you see joy.
When you frown, you see worry.
What you feel inside is what you see outside."

Leo placed his hand against the cool bark.

"So, if I feel kind… the world looks kinder?"

The tree shimmered.
"Yes. Your heart is the light that colors what you see."

Leo took a deep breath and smiled again.
The forest seemed brighter.

Tiny Truth

"The light I see in the world begins inside me."

Parent & Child Reflection

- Ask softly:
  "When do you feel proud of yourself?"

- Try together:
  Stand in front of a mirror and each say one kind thing about yourselves.

- Reassure:
  "Loving yourself helps you see love everywhere."

The Invisible Wings

In a wide green meadow lived a caterpillar named Nora.

Every day, Nora watched the butterflies float through the air, their wings painting colors across the sky.

"I wish I could fly," Nora sighed.
"But I don't have wings."

A wise grasshopper nearby chuckled softly.
"You do," he said. "You just can't see them yet."

Nora laughed.
"That's silly. If I had wings, I'd feel them."

"Not everything shows itself right away," the grasshopper replied.
"Some things grow in quiet."

So, Nora began to imagine.

She imagined wind lifting her.
She imagined light unfolding behind her back.
She imagined herself brave enough to trust what she couldn't see.

One day, Nora felt tired and wrapped herself in a soft, silky cocoon.

Inside the stillness, she whispered,
"I don't see my wings… but I believe in them."

Time passed.

And when Nora finally stretched again, something gentle opened behind her.

Wings.

Golden, light, and strong.

As she lifted into the sky, she realized something important:

She had been growing wings long before she ever flew.

Tiny Truth

"Even when I can't see my wings, they are growing."

Parent & Child Reflection

- Ask gently:
  "What's something you're learning or becoming right now?"

- Try together:
  Draw or imagine invisible wings and name what they're made of (kindness, courage, curiosity, patience).

- Reassure:
  "You don't have to rush becoming. You are already on your way."

Closing of Part II — Wings

These stories are seeds.

They are meant to be read more than once,
felt more than explained,
and remembered long after childhood.

Children who grow up with stories like these learn something essential:

That who they are is enough.
That feelings are safe.
That growth happens in its own time.
That light does not need permission to shine.

And sometimes, as you read these stories aloud,
you may notice something inside you soften too.

That is the child within you remembering their wings.

The Magic We Make Together

Shared Rituals, Practices, and Everyday Sacred Moments

Love Made Visible

Children don't remember advice the way they remember experiences.

They remember:

- how it felt to be listened to
- how calm returned after big feelings
- how laughter lived in the ordinary
- how love showed up consistently

This section is not about doing everything.
It's about choosing **a few moments** and letting them matter.

The practices that follow are invitations, not expectations.
You don't need special tools.
You don't need extra time.

What you need is already here:
your presence, your attention, and your willingness to slow down together.

Magic doesn't arrive loudly.
It arrives quietly — through repetition, rhythm, and care.

Practice One

The Joy Jar

Remembering What Feels Good

Purpose:
Gratitude, emotional awareness, memory-building

How it works:
Keep a jar, bowl, or box somewhere visible.

Each day (or whenever it feels right), invite everyone to write or draw:

- one moment of joy
- one thing they're grateful for
- one small win

Drop it into the jar.

Once a week or once a month, open it together and read them aloud.

Why it matters:
Joy spoken aloud becomes anchored in the nervous system.
Children learn that good moments are worth noticing — even on hard days.

Gentle phrase to use:
"We keep the good things where we can find them."

Practice Two

Morning Magic Minutes

Starting the Day Connected

Purpose:
Grounding, intention-setting, emotional safety

How it works:
Before leaving the house (or before starting the day):

1.   Everyone stands or sits together.
2.   Take one slow breath in and out.
3.   Choose a "word of the day"
     (kindness, calm, courage, patience).
4.   End with a hug, high-five, or smile.

This takes less than one minute.

Why it matters:
Children who begin the day connected carry that sense of safety with them.
The nervous system learns: I am not alone.

Gentle phrase to use:
"We start together. We return together."

The Emotional Weather Check

Learning to Name Feelings Without Fixing Them

Purpose:
Emotional literacy, empathy, self-awareness

How it works:
Invite everyone to describe how they feel using weather language:

- sunny
- cloudy
- stormy
- mixed

No fixing. No correcting.
Just noticing.

You might say:
"Thank you for telling me."

Why it matters:
Children learn that feelings are safe to name — and that they don't need to be solved immediately.

This builds emotional confidence.

Gentle phrase to use:
"All weather passes."

Practice Four

The Candle of Calm

Returning to Peace After Big Feelings

Purpose:
Co-regulation, emotional repair

How it works:
Keep a candle (or battery light) in a safe place.

When emotions feel big, anyone can ask for "candle time."

Light it.
Sit quietly.
Take three slow breaths together.

Blow it out when calm returns.

Why it matters:
This teaches children that calm is something we come back to, not something we demand.

Gentle phrase to use:
"Peace begins here."

Practice Five

The Feather of Truth

Listening With the Whole Body

Purpose:
Communication, respect, patience

How it works:
Use a feather, stone, or small object.

Only the person holding it speaks.
Everyone else listens.

When finished, pass it along.

This works beautifully for:

- family meetings
- bedtime check-ins
- resolving conflict

Why it matters:
Children feel heard without interruption.
Listening becomes an act of love.

Gentle phrase to use:

"I'm listening."

Practice Six

The Energy Reset

Observing Without Absorbing

Purpose:
Empath awareness, boundary-building

How it works:
After busy days or emotional events:

1. Shake arms and legs gently.
2. Take a deep breath in.
3. Exhale slowly.
4. Say together:
   "I send back what is not mine."
   "I keep my own peace."

Why it matters:
This reinforces the lesson that empathy does not require carrying everything.

Gentle phrase to use:
"I can care and still stay me."

Heart-to-Heart Repair

Teaching That Love Returns

Purpose:
Repair, trust, emotional resilience

How it works:
After a disagreement or hard moment, sit together and share:

- one thing you're sorry for
- one thing you appreciate
- one thing you love about each other

Keep it simple.

Why it matters:
Children learn that conflict does not threaten connection.

Gentle phrase to use:
"We always find our way back."

The Nature Return

Grounding Through the Living World

Purpose:
Regulation, embodiment, reverence for life

How it works:
Spend intentional time outdoors — even briefly.

Invite your child to:

- place their hands on a tree
- sit or lie on the ground
- watch clouds move
- notice birds, wind, or sunlight

No lesson required.

Why it matters:
Nature regulates the nervous system without effort.
Children remember that they belong to something larger than worry.

Gentle phrase to use:
"The earth holds us."

Practice Nine

The Moon Check-In

Honoring Cycles and Emotional Change

Purpose:
Emotional awareness, rhythm, acceptance of change

How it works:
On the full moon or new moon:

- share one thing you're ready to release
- share one thing you're inviting in

This can be spoken, drawn, or written.

No ritual tools needed.

Why it matters:
Children learn that change is natural and emotions move in cycles.

Gentle phrase to use:
"It's okay to let things change."

Practice Ten

Creative Release Time

Letting Feelings Move Through Art

Purpose:
Expression, processing, self-trust

How it works:
Offer art supplies with no goal:

- crayons
- clay
- paint
- movement
- music

Invite your child to create what the feeling feels like — not what it "should" look like.

Do not interpret unless invited.

Why it matters:
Children learn that feelings don't need explanation to be valid.

Gentle phrase to use:
"Show me what it feels like."

The Gratitude Walk

Training the Eye to Notice Goodness

Purpose:
Perspective, joy, mindfulness

How it works:
Take a walk and take turns naming things you appreciate:

- colors
- textures
- sounds
- small surprises

No correction. No competition.

Why it matters:
Gratitude practiced physically becomes embodied, not forced.

Gentle phrase to use:
"Look at what we noticed."

Practice Twelve

The Boundary Practice

Learning to Say Yes and No With Confidence

Purpose:
Self-respect, empowerment, leadership

How it works:
Practice saying:

- "Yes, please."
- "No, thank you."
- "I need help."
- "I need space."

Turn it into a game or role-play.

Why it matters:
Children learn that boundaries are allowed — and respected.

Gentle phrase to use:
"My voice matters."

The End-of-Day Release

Putting the Day Down Gently

Purpose:
Sleep readiness, nervous system settling

How it works:
At bedtime, invite your child to:

- name one thing they're done carrying
- name one thing they want to remember

End with a breath or quiet moment.

Why it matters:
Children sleep better when the day is emotionally closed.

Gentle phrase to use:
"We rest now."

The Family Identity Statement

Strengthening Belonging and Values

Purpose:
Belonging, clarity, shared meaning

How it works:
Create a short family statement together, such as:

- "In this family, we try again."
- "In this family, we speak kindly."
- "In this family, we take care of our hearts."

Display it somewhere visible.

Why it matters:
Children feel safer when values are clear and lived.

Gentle phrase to use:
"This is who we are."

Practice Fifteen

The Listening Pause

Teaching That Silence Is Also Communication

Purpose:
Presence, respect, nervous system regulation

How it works:
Sit quietly together for one minute.
No talking.
No fixing.
Just being.

This can be done:

- after conflict
- before transitions
- before sleep

Why it matters:
Children learn that stillness is safe — not empty.

Gentle phrase to use:
"We're here."

Closing Note for Parents

You are not meant to carry these practices perfectly.
They are seeds, not rules — offered gently, meant to grow in their own time.

Choose what feels alive.
Release what feels heavy.

Children do not learn most from what is done occasionally with effort,
but from what is repeated with love.

Each time you pause instead of rush,
repair instead of retreat,
breathe instead of react,
or listen instead of explain —
you are teaching something no book ever could.

You don't need to practice everything here.
Choose what fits your family now.
Let it change as your family changes.
Return when you forget.

That returning is the practice.

When love is repeated gently,
children grow up knowing that feelings are safe,
repair is possible,
and presence matters.

These are the roots that hold them steady.
These are the wings that help them rise.

Final Integration & Closing Blessing

For the Roots You've Strengthened and the Wings You've Trusted

There comes a moment when a book ends —
but what it points to continues.

It continues in the pauses you take before responding.
In the way you soften instead of harden.
In the nights you repair instead of retreat.
In the mornings you begin again.

This book was never meant to give you more to do.
It was meant to help you remember what you already know.

That children are not here to be shaped by our fears,
but guided by our love.

That they are not empty vessels, but souls arriving with their own wisdom, timing, and light.

And that parenting is not about perfection —
it is about presence, humility, and courage.

You have not been asked to erase your past.
Only to tend it with care, so what grows next can be rooted in truth instead of survival.

Each time you choose awareness over habit,
you loosen the grip of old patterns.

Each time you choose connection over control,
you create safety where there once may have been silence.

Each time you choose to see your child as a whole being —
not an extension of you, not a reflection of your wounds —
you honor the sacred responsibility you were entrusted with.

And yes, entrusted is the right word.

Because whether you believe it symbolically, spiritually, or intuitively,
there is something meaningful in the idea that children arrive on purpose.

That they choose — or are guided toward —
the families who will shape them, challenge them, and love them into becoming.

Not because you are perfect.
But because you are willing.

Willing to grow.
Willing to listen.
Willing to heal where healing is asked of you.

Your child does not need to understand you.
It is not their job to carry your story.

Your work is to carry yourself —
with honesty, compassion, and steadiness —
so your child is free to carry their own.

To the parent reading this:
may you release the weight of doing it "right."

May you trust that showing up — again and again — is enough.

To the child listening nearby, or the child still living within you:
may you always know that your feelings are welcome,
your voice matters,
and your light was never accidental.

May your home be a place where mistakes soften into repair,
where laughter lives beside tears,
and where love is practiced more often than it is perfected.

May your family grow strong roots —
roots of safety, truth, and belonging.

And may those roots support wide, trusting wings —
wings that rise without fear,
that explore without losing themselves,
that return without shame.

This is how cycles change.
This is how light continues.

Not through grand gestures,
but through everyday love,
offered gently,
and lived fully.

www.ingramcontent.com/pod-product-compliance
Lightning Source LLC
Chambersburg PA
CBHW051627140626
46547CB00033B/2769